The purpose of this study guide is to provide supplemental educational material. It is not intended as a substitute or replacement of THE NICKEL BOYS.

Published by SuperSummary, www.supersummary.com

ISBN – 9798693443068

For more information or to learn about our complete library of study guides, please visit http://www.supersummary.com

Please submit any comments, corrections, or questions to: http://www.supersummary.com/support/

TABLE OF CONTENTS

Like his 2016 bestseller, *The Underground Railroad*, Colson Whitehead's *The Nickel Boys* (2019) won the Pulitzer Prize for Fiction (Whitehead is only the fourth writer in history to win two Pulitzers). *The Nickel Boys* describes life in a reform school from the point of view of young Black teenager. Whitehead based Nickel Academy on the real life Dozier School, a Florida facility that ran for over a century, until a university investigation publicized its racist and abusive practices.

In addition to two Pulitzers, Whitehead is also the recipient of a MacArthur Fellowship (2002) and a Guggenheim Fellowship (2013). NPR called Whitehead "one of the most gifted novelists in America today."

Plot Summary

The Nickel Boys recounts the life of Elwood Curtis, an African American boy growing up in Florida during the early years of the Civil Rights movement. Elwood, who lives with his grandmother, is dutiful, industrious, and filled with idealism. He excels in school, works hard, and has a strong support network of teachers, his employer, and his grandmother, who envision a bright future for young Elwood. Their hopes seem fulfilled when Elwood gets into a local Black college, where he will take advanced classes available to high-achieving high school students. The college is far from Elwood's home, so he decides to hitch a ride rather than walking the seven miles. After a man driving a stolen car picks him up, a police officer pulls them over. Elwood is implicated in the theft, and a judge sentences him to time in Nickel Academy, a notorious institution for juvenile offenders.

Elwood decides to keep his head down, stay out of trouble, and simply survive until he's served his time. He befriends Turner, a more experienced boy who sees Elwood as naïve, but admires his optimism and devotion to social justice. However, Elwood cannot repress his innate desire to right wrongs. When he defends a smaller boy from bullies, he learns that noble gestures have no place in Nickel. The sadistic superintendent Spenser takes Elwood, the bullies, and their victim to the White House (a small shed near the dormitories), where he beats them severely with a leather strap. The beating changes Elwood. At first, he is cowed. He has nightmares, and the slightest sounds trigger his memory of the strap. Over time, however, he grows angry, and his sense of justice kicks in. Griff, the bully who has victimized many of Nickel's weaker Black boys, fails to take a dive in a fixed boxing match that the superintendent and townspeople bet on, he is quietly taken out to the whipping post and is never seen again.

While on Community Service detail with Turner, Elwood realizes that Nickel's administration is committing fraud against the state of Florida by selling resources earmarked for Black students to local businesses. He keeps meticulous records of each delivery, hoping to reveal the corruption to someone who can make a difference. He resolves to see those responsible pay a price for his beating, for the general atmosphere of terror and abuse, and for the misappropriation of funds that fuels discrepancies between the segregated White and Black facilities at Nickel.

When state inspectors arrive to review Nickel's legal compliance, Elwood is unable to deliver his evidence, and entrusts Turner to do it for him. Turner betrays him, however, and turns the evidence over to Spencer, the sadistic superintendent who drags Elwood to the White House once again. After another cruel beating, Elwood is locked in solitary confinement, where he begins to lose hope. Throughout the novel, there are sporadic glimpses of the future: Elwood living in New York, and eventually finding success as a business owner and happiness as a married man. Elwood, it seems, has managed to prosper, despite the ghosts of his past.

Back at Nickel, Turner rescues Elwood from solitary, and they flee during the night. Spencer and his subordinates spot them riding stolen bicycles along a county road. When Turner and Elwood run across a pasture toward the cover of nearby woods, Spencer and his men jump out of the van and shoot at the fleeing boys. Turner escapes into the woods, but Elwood is killed. Whitehead then reveals that the man who calls himself Elwood Curtis in the glimpses into the future is actually Turner. Turner took Elwood's identity as a survival strategy and a tribute to his dead friend. In the end, with Nickel's unmarked graves excavated by researchers into its horrible history, Turner takes one final trip down to Florida to tell the world about Nickel, and to seek a final measure of justice for Elwood.

Prologue-Chapter 3

Prologue Summary

On an abandoned lot in south Florida, near a cemetery known as Boot Hill, an archaeology student discovers a series of unmarked graves. Before the lot can be developed as planned, the bodies must be identified and resettled, and the arduous legal process completed. Archaeology students discover 43 bodies, seven of which are never identified. The unmarked graves sit on the site of a former reform school with a mysterious and brutal past filled with trauma.

The school's survivors call themselves the Nickel Boys. The Boys meet annually for a "strange and necessary" reunion during which they share stories of their past and their present (7). When the old gravesite is unearthed, the memories flood back, and one former Nickel Boy, Elwood Curtis, decides to confront his past.

Chapter 1 Summary

In 1962, a young Elwood Curtis receives for Christmas an album, *Martin Luther King at Zion Hill,* and through King's words, Elwood experiences the past abuse and the future salvation of Black people. King's words give Elwood self-esteem in a world that devalues him.

Elwood lives with his grandmother Harriet, a house cleaner at the Richmond Hotel in the Tallahassee neighborhood of Frenchtown. His parents are alive, but no longer involved in his life. While Harriet cleans rooms, the hotel kitchen staff watches over Elwood. One day, when Elwood is 12, a busboy finds a set of encyclopedias left behind in one of the rooms. Pete, a dishwasher, challenges Elwood to a dish-drying contest for sole ownership of the leather-bound reference books. The contest is a prank—something the restaurant staff does often to get Elwood to do their work for them. Elwood "wins" by a single plate. But, after dragging the books home and placing them on his grandmother's bookshelves, he finds that only the first volume is a real book. All the rest are blank—stand-ins used by traveling salesmen, his grandmother speculates. Elwood keeps the volumes anyway, but leaves the kitchen—he finally sees the staff's mean-spirited pranks.

Chapter 2 Summary

In the immediate aftermath of *Brown vs. Board of Education,* Elwood wonders when he will see other Black people as guests of The Richmond rather than just employees. In the meantime, White business owners in the neighborhood see Elwood as more industrious and trustworthy than most of the other boys; at 13, he begins working at Marconi's tobacco shop and newsstand. The White Italian-American Marconi started the store after WWII as a place for Black soldiers to buy condoms and tobacco; since then, Marconi has rebranded as a more family-friendly establishment, selling candy and comic books.

Harriet keeps half of Elwood's salary and saves the other half for Elwood's college fund. As an employee, Elwood shows initiative, suggesting Black newspapers Marconi should keep in stock, remembering which vendors shortchanged the store, and acting as a mediator between Marconi and the neighborhood women who don't trust him. When he has time to browse, Elwood witnesses the civil rights struggle happening across the United States in the vivid photographs of *Life* magazine, and longs to join the fight.

Elwood differs with his boss on the subject of shoplifting. Marconi looks the other way, resigned to kids swiping candy as normal mischief. To chase every kid who stole a candy bar, he reasons, would be bad for business; but Elwood can't countenance boys he knows stealing from his employer. One day, he calls Marconi's attention to two boys from the neighborhood trying to steal candy. Later that night, on his way home, they jump Elwood and beat him, to teach him a lesson. The words of Dr. King, however, give Elwood a sense of dignity when "there are small forces that want to keep you down" (27).

Chapter 3 Summary

Mr. Hill, Elwood's history teacher at the all-Black Lincoln High School, is the first to acknowledge that the second-hand textbooks the students receive from the nearby White school are not only out of date, but are filled with racist slurs scrawled by White students. Hill asks Elwood and the other students to go through their books and cross out all of the handwritten nastiness with black marker. Elwood is shocked that no one has ever thought to do this before.

Hill teaches post-Civil War history with a generous helping of contemporary context, regaling his students with tales of his freedom rides and lunch counter sit-ins. The studious Elwood is a favorite among the Lincoln faculty, who for three years cast him as Thomas Jackson—the Black statesman who informs Florida's slaves they have been freed—in the school Emancipation Play.

As the civil rights movement makes its way to Frenchtown, Elwood is eager to join, but Harriet disapproves. She knows what happens to Black people who confront the system to demand their equal share. Despite his grandmother's prohibition, however, Elwood takes the day off work and joins a group of Florida A&M students picketing the local movie theater. In the picket line, he encounters Hill and a few Lincoln High seniors. Inspired by the social justice movement, Elwood eagerly awaits college, where he will find his place within its ranks.

Elwood's involvement in civil rights has given him a newfound confidence, and he makes friends with Peter Coombs. Harriet deems Peter a worthy friend because "he played violin and shared a bookish bent with her grandson" (38).

That summer, Hill gives Elwood a copy of James Baldwin's Notes of a Native Son (a compilation of essays about race in America and Europe). Inspired, Elwood writes letters to activist newspapers, managing to get one published. At the end of the summer, Hill offers Elwood the opportunity to take free college-level classes at Melvin Griggs Technical, "the colored college just south of Tallahassee" (39), seven miles away from Frenchtown.

To get there for his first day, Elwood hitches a ride from a man named Rodney. A state trooper pulls Rodney over for driving a stolen car.

Prologue-Chapter 3 Analysis

The young, idealistic Elwood of the novel's early chapters contrasts with the jaded, older self of the Prologue, embittered from his abusive experience at Nickel. Because the innocent Elwood Curtis—an earnest and studious young Black boy growing up in Jim Crow-era Florida— will ultimately end up in the infamous Nickel Reform

School, guilty of simply being in the wrong place at the wrong time, the division between past and future selves points to the effect of racism. Even Elwood's seemingly strong support network—his grandmother, his boss, his high school history teacher—and his invitation to enroll in free college courses are not enough to keep him out of the clutches of Jim Crow-era racial inequity. However, since Elwood in the past is actually a different person from Elwood in the present, Whitehead suggests an even darker reading: that survival in that harsh period depended on a more cynical take on the world—idealists like Elwood, eager to explore the Civil Rights movement and his place within it, were mowed down by the racist machine.

As the United States in the present confronts its failures with civil rights yet again, trying to rectify the violence visited on so many Black people by the police, Whitehead reminds us of the unresolved history that has brought us to this moment. When the White state trooper pulls Rodney over, Rodney tries to distance himself from Elwood, knowing that the consequences of guilt-by-association could be severe for this college-bound young man. Rodney's fears are realized when Elwood is sentenced to time in Nickel Academy, and everything he has worked for is shattered for no other reason than his mere proximity to a crime. The bald unfairness and the helplessness of anyone in Elwood's orbit to intervene is a rebuke to a White supremacist system upheld by White people who often do not even acknowledge benefitting from it.

Chapters 4-6

Chapter 4 Summary

Chained alongside two White boys, Elwood is arrested and transported to Nickel Academy. At first glance, Nickel appears no different from a college campus: well-maintained grounds, red brick buildings, shade trees. Like other schools, Nickel is segregated: some buildings are for the White boys and others for Black boys. Inside the Academy, the boys are reassured that Nickel is simply a school with a staff of teachers. Superintendent Maynard Spencer lays out the rules—boys who apply themselves, stay out of trouble, and focus on their studies achieve the rank of Ace and can leave to return to their families. Implicit in these rules is a severe threat to those not obeying the rules.

Elwood tries to take some hope from the fact that the dormitory's house father Blakeley is an older Black man, assuming "the black staff looked after their own" (50). Walking Elwood to his dormitory, Blakeley explains the rules: All boys are required to attend school and to work, to learn responsibility and sustainable life skills. The dormitories, however, present a different reality from the trees and manicured lawns: threadbare and fraying linens, peeling paint, graffiti. Lying in bed that night, Elwood hears a horrible mechanical sound and cries himself to sleep, wondering how fate has landed him in this place.

Chapter 5 Summary

Nickel's morning rituals include attendance, two-minute cold showers in water that "smelled of rotten eggs" (55), and finally, breakfast. In the dining hall, Elwood meets Turner, a boy strangely "a part and apart" (57) of any situation. He also encounters Griff, Lonnie, and Black Mike, a threatening trio of bullies the other boys know to avoid. After breakfast, Elwood's dormmate Desmond escorts him to the classroom, although academic performance doesn't carry much weight at Nickel. More important, Desmond informs him, is earning merits through following the rules and not making trouble.

Inside the classroom, Elwood is shocked to find outdated textbooks written for elementary school students. After class, he inquires about advanced classes, and the apathetic instructor vows to ask Director Hardee, the head of Nickel, about it.

Later, Elwood rakes leaves and maintains the grounds as part of the yard crew. The leader of this crew is Jaime, a Mexican-American boy whose light brown skin confuses the White supremacist segregationists who run Nickel. In the summer, when Jaime gets a tan, Spencer moves him to the Black side of Nickel, but in the winter, Director Hardee shuffles him back to the White side. A small hill separates the "colored dormitory" from Boot Hill, an old graveyard marked by white crosses and "bent and lurching trees" (62). On his rounds, Elwood sees a small, rust-covered building between the White and Black dormitories; he is warned to stay away.

After work detail, Elwood tours the sparsely equipped rec room. He learns about house captains—peers assigned to monitor other boys' behavior. One day, Elwood sees Lonnie and Black Mike bullying a younger boy. When he tries to intervene, Black Mike slugs him across the jaw. A guard who walks in on the scene calls the boys the n-word and tells them to expect to hear from Spencer.

Chapter 6 Summary

That night, Spencer and a houseman named Earl load Lonnie, Black Mike, Elwood, and Corey, the bullies' victim, into two brown Chevys bound for the White House, the small rusty building Elwood was warned to avoid.

Before they go, Desmond warns Elwood not to struggle against the beating—the buckled strap the guards use is barbed to rip the skin with each strike if the victim moves.

Inside, Spencer and Earl viciously beat the boys one by one. Elwood cannot hear the sounds of the beatings—all he hears is the same loud mechanical noise that he'd heard his first night at Nickel. He tries counting the seconds each boy is in the room to prepare for how long his punishment will be, but soon realizes that there is no rhyme or reason for how many lashes each boy receives, no sense of fairness or justice. The larger boys, the bullies, each are beaten for 28 seconds, while the tiny Corey—their victim—receives 70 seconds. The only thing driving Spencer is rage— after he tells the boys to take their beatings and shut their mouths, Corey received the most lashes because he cannot stop crying.

In the room where the beating takes place, Elwood sees a blood-spattered mattress and an enormous industrial fan— the source of the mechanical noise that drowns out the boys' screams. This keeps up the façade that Nickel adheres to Florida laws, which ban corporal punishment. Elwood passes out before his punishment is over.

Chapters 4-6 Analysis

Elwood has grown up believing that hard work and good behavior earn rewards—a supportive community, an offer of. Of course, his opportunities have been limited by racism and the white supremacist system, but his perseverance in school results in the offer of free college classes, while his upright conduct gets him a good job and the respect of Mr. Marconi. Elwood is committed to a high standard of behavior and a code of ethics, both of which find support in the speeches of Dr. King. In general, though he has felt the effects of segregation and Jim Crow—second-hand textbooks scrawled with racial epithets, angry looks from Whites as he walks a picket line, his grandmother's fear of White people—he moves past these incidents with the belief that the Civil Rights movement will bring change and transformation.

In Nickel, however, Elwood suddenly experiences the radical unfairness of racial injustice firsthand. The learning component of Nickel Academy is utterly perfunctory; the facilities are segregated and not at all equal; and punishment is meted out in a brutally random fashion: Elwood is punished alongside two bullies for trying to break up a fight. Nickel's pretense of reform is a sham; in reality, the punitive institution lays open the horror of white supremacy and for-profit incarceration, describing the beginnings of the school-to-prison pipeline.

Elwood is completely unprepared for what lies beyond the red brick walls and stately cedar and beech trees. Whitehead walks his readers through Elwood's experience dispassionately for maximum impact. He eschews subjective descriptions of the beating—how Elwood screams or how the strap feels as it tears into his flesh—to avoid turning the novel into titillating, sensationalistic horror. Rather, Whitehead documents evidence: a stark, chilling description of the noise of an industrial fan used to drown out the boys' cries; the sight of dried blood splattered on the wall; and Elwood passing out mid-beating. Our imagination empathetically fills in the gaps, putting us into Elwood's place for a ruthless glimpse into one young man's descent into the pit of racial injustice.

Chapters 7-9

Chapter 7 Summary

Elwood's grandmother Harriet comes to visit him in Nickel, but the staff tell her that he is ill and cannot see visitors. Harriet is no stranger to death and loss. Her father, jailed for not stepping out of the way of a White woman, was found hanged in his cell; her husband was killed in a bar fight; and Elwood's parents left town in the middle of the night without saying goodbye. Harriet's mission now is to free Elwood from Nickel.

Elwood lies in the Nickel infirmary bed recovering from his injuries and dreaming about his release. The doctor has to pick pieces of his pant fabric out of his skin and wounds—it had become embedded there during the whipping. The sick White patients, Elwood notices, receive preferential treatment over the Black ones, though doctor's remedy for all ailments is aspirin.

Reading a history of Nickel Academy, Elwood realizes its credo and its actual practice are two starkly different things. In operation for over 60 years, Nickel was founded as a place to reform young offenders and provide them with a moral compass and practical life skills. In reality, the boys' free labor turns a profit for the institution, an incentive to keep them imprisoned rather than reforming and releasing them. The school earns $250,000 a year from its printing press and runs a brickworks that produces 20,000 bricks a year, which are sold nation-wide.

Elwood shares the ward with Turner, who occasionally avoids work detail by eating soap powder to make himself sick. There is one other boy there: a silent, mysterious presence hidden behind a folding screen. The doctor and nurse treat him with great care, reading and singing to him at night.

When Elwood mentions he has a lawyer working on his case, Turner tells him "you already got off lucky" (80) for simply surviving the beating. Some boys who go down to the White House never return. Turner also explains that what Elwood thought was bullying was actually a sexual game that Elwood should not have interrupted: The bullies beat up Corey, who then performs oral sex on them. Turner believes all of this is consensual; Elwood disagrees.

Elwood declares that the boys should protest the flagrant illegality of the beatings, but Turner is a pragmatist: Morals can get a boy killed. Elwood resolves to play by the rules and simply survive, but the scars from his beating make it hard for him to repress his sense of justice. When his grandmother returns, Elwood wants to tell her about the White House and his beating, but he cannot bring himself to break her heart with the information.

Chapter 8 Summary

Released from the hospital, Elwood is assigned to the yard crew again. He decides to do his best to rack up enough merits to leave Nickel by the following June. That way, he can still go to college, and will have missed only one year of school. He worries that Harriet has spent all of their savings on a lawyer—Mr. Anderson, an idealistic young White man from the North eager to make a difference.

One day, while cleaning out the schoolhouse basement, he discovers a collection of classic British literature (Dickens, Trollope, etc.). He realizes his Nickel Academy classes will never challenge him, so he reads these books on his own. Meanwhile, Desmond educates Elwood in the logic (or illogic) of the merit/demerit system. Elwood tries to figure out a calculus for early release, but the system is completely arbitrary: Staying out of trouble won't help if trouble finds you, Desmond says. Despite the odds, Elwood resolves to leave early and set his life back on track.

One day, Elwood is reassigned to a Community Service detail with Turner and a young White Nickel employee named Harper. Harper's mother worked at Nickel, and he grew up around the school. Because of this, he sees the boys as unluckier versions of himself and isn't malicious towards them.

Community service, it turns out, involves selling the provisions issued to the school by the Florida government to local businesses—Nickel administrators shortchange the students and pocket the profits. Still, this work allows Elwood to be away from Nickel for a few hours, and he relishes the freedom, but Turner warns Elwood to keep quiet about the details of the job. After they complete their deliveries one afternoon, Harper leaves Turner and Elwood to paint the gazebo of a local White woman. Community Service often means doing menial labor like this for highly placed townspeople and for Spencer's patrons and cronies.

While working, Turner tells Elwood his backstory. He worked as a pinsetter at a bowling alley, joking and entertaining the White customers until a Black fry cook accuses him of "shucking and jiving for these white people" (95). The criticism stung, and Turner's attitude turned sullen and angry. One night, he retaliated against an angry customer by smashing his car window.

Elwood is placed permanently on Community Service detail. The new job lifts his spirits, and he keeps meticulous records of every delivery.

Chapter 9 Summary

Griff, the feared bully and "baddest brother on campus" (98), is chosen to represent the Black side of Nickel in the annual wintertime Black vs. White boxing match. Trevor Nickel, the school's founder, who got the job because of his Ku Klux Klan affiliation and despite never having run a school before, instituted the boxing tradition as a way to build moral character through physical fitness (and to have sexual access to the young boys in the showers, abuse the school's current psychologist also perpetuates).

Griff's seeming invincibility fills the Black boys with glee—he should easily be able to best the White boys' contender, Big Chet. However, Turner overhears Superintendent Spencer order Griff to throw the fight or else be taken "out back." According to Turner, "out back" means being shackled to two iron rings deeply embedded in two trees behind the laundry building, where guards horsewhip you, and then "[T]hey put you down as escaped and that's that, boy" (105). Being disappeared like this is a punishment reserved only for the Black boys. Elwood has trouble believing this could work—wouldn't the boys' families demand answers? Turner scoffs that not everyone has Elwood's support system; he has brought Elwood to the iron rings to show him the true nature of Nickel.

The town's White residents eagerly attend the boxing match between Griff and Big Chet. The audience puts bets on the outcome, heavily favoring Griff. Spencer has promised the school's board of directors to rig the right, so they can bet against Griff and make lots of money.

Griff has been crowing about his upcoming chances, and the boys' admiration has turned his head the last few days. Elwood wonders whether Griff is smart enough to remember to lose. Sure enough, caught up in the fight, Griff misses the right time to go down. He wins the fight during the third round, and then, confused and terrified of the consequences, pleads with Spencer that he made a mistake—he thought they were still in the second round of the fight, not the third. That night, Spencer and other guards take Griff "out back," and he never returns. The boys mythologize him, saying that he refused to lose as a matter of principle and that he managed to escape.

In the present, student archeologists find and exhume the body of Griff, whose wrists were broken, showing that he must have been manacled while being beaten to death. The iron rings remain in the trees, though few people now know what purpose they used to serve.

Chapters 7-9 Analysis

These chapters reveal the full truth behind the abuses that take place at Nickel: the town of Eleanor, Florida, profits so much from the graft and thievery taking place at Nickel that no one will ever protest its abuses. The financial malfeasance works like this: Florida issues food and other supplies to Nickel on the taxpayers' dime, and then Spencer steals a large fraction of the food and supplies intended for the Black half of Nickel and sells it at cut rates to Eleanor businesses. The owners of those businesses, and anyone else with political power in Eleanor, also get to use the Black boys as free labor. This self-perpetuating system reaches its apotheosis each year during the boxing match where spectators bet on the outcome—an outcome already rigged and predetermined by the same powerful elite. The boys' lives and potential are only worth the profit the town can exploit from them. Those who upset the system, like Griff, are killed without consequences.

Elwood, ever academic, decides to become a student of this system. Although his first trip to the White House has taught him to keep his head down, Whitehead hints that Elwood's stubborn streak of righteousness remains. Elwood keeps meticulous notes on every delivery he and Turner make; and Whitehead leaves open the possibility that Elwood is waiting for the right moment to expose Nickel's corruption. Years of listening to Civil Rights icons have instilled in him a strong moral compass that even the threat of punishment cannot erase.

For the other Black boys at Nickel, who don't have a full grasp of the system within which they are trapped, the boxing match is a potent locus of hope. They believe that if Griff wins, he will prove them equal to the White boys—if only for that night. This racial solidarity transcends all else. It doesn't matter that Griff has been their tormentor; now, he is their savior, and his victory something to hold onto during the misery of incarceration.

Chapters 10-13

Chapter 10 Summary

Christmas at Nickel involves elaborate holiday displays that attract visitors not only from Florida but from neighboring states as well. When Desmond finds a small can of horse medicine inside a maintenance shed, Jaime suggests spiking a supervisor's drink with it. The boys indulge their fantasies about which abusive staff member to give it to, and they tentatively decide on Earl, an alcoholic who has some mysterious past conflict with Jaime. Jaime is the most enthusiastic about this plan, arguing that the staff holiday luncheon would be the perfect time to execute it. In the end, however, the boys decide the plan is too risky, and they abandon it.

One afternoon, after completing their Community Service rounds in Eleanor, Harper briefly leaves Turner and Elwood alone to wander unsupervised down Main Street. They engage in a hypothetical discussion about escape: What would be the best way to do it? Turner has a plan: he would steal clothes from a clothesline, raid a house they've made deliveries to for supplies, make his way south instead of north, and, most importantly, he would go alone— another boy would only hinder him. Turner's life is not so different from other Nickel boys: absentee father, deceased mother. After the kindly aunt raising him fell into an abusive relationship, he ran away.

Returning to Nickel, they find out that Earl is in the hospital, having been dosed with the horse medicine. A trail of blood leads from the staff dining room towards the infirmary. Both Desmond and Jaime deny responsibility, but Jaime's sly smile reveals that he is the one who poisoned Earl.

The culprit is never discovered, and the boys breathe a collective sigh of relief. Later that day, Elwood and Turner sit on a hill admiring the Christmas lights and imagining a more hopeful future. What they don't realize is that Earl is immediately replaced with Hennepin, a much more vicious and brutal guard.

Chapter 11 Summary

Flashing forward to 1968, Elwood is now living in New York City. Manhattan is in the throes of an oppressive summer coupled with a garbage strike that fills the streets with an overpowering stench and hordes of rats. Elwood remembers first coming to Manhattan and renting a room in a flophouse where he began cleaning simply because no one else would.

He works as a mover, although lifting heavy furniture has left him with a bad back. He shares an apartment with his girlfriend Denise, an ESL teacher at a school for continuing education where Elwood completes his GED. While proud of his accomplishment, this is an older and more jaded Elwood, one whose politics favor any position that "stuck it to the man, rule one" (141).

With money saved from his moving job, Elwood buys a van and starts his own moving company, Ace Moving. He thinks that he picked the name so it would come early in the alphabetical phone book listings, but realizes that he must have subconsciously named after the Nickel term for freedom.

Chapter 12 Summary

There are four ways out of Nickel: early release due to good behavior or age (Nickel is required to release boys when they turn 18); legal intervention; death (administrative records are inconsistent on numbers and causes); and finally, escape (although the consequences of being caught are severe). Those who plausibly died of natural causes are buried on Boot Hill, and others are buried in unmarked graves around the property.

One legendary escapee was Clayton Smith, a boy with neither the physical skills nor the constitution to endure Nickel's torments. Running after being sexually abused by a house father, Smith first made his way along country roads and through dark woods under cover of darkness, finally stealing clothes and deciding to hitchhike. A seemingly kind White man in a Packard picked him up, and Smith imagined himself a safe distance away, until the Packard drove him right back to Nickel. Smith paid for his escape with his life.

As his time passes at Nickel, Elwood realizes that compliance and a low profile, while keeping him out of the White House, have drained his spirit and his dignity. Harriet can see this during her visits, and she finds it hard to return to Nickel only to watch Elwood falling further into despair. One Sunday while Harriet is visiting, she informs her grandson that Mr. Anderson, the lawyer who had been working on Elwood's legal appeal, has absconded with Harriet's $200 retainer. Elwood assures Harriet he doesn't blame her, but he fixes his mind on a fifth way out: "Get rid of Nickel" (158).

Chapter 13 Summary

Back in New York, 1988, Elwood watches the New York City Marathon, rooting for the stragglers, the runners who barely make it across the finish line but still persevere.

After the race, he runs into a former Nickel Boy, Chickie Pete. Following his release from Nickel, Chickie served in the military. After discharge, Chickie worked a variety of jobs and drank too much. After a bar fight, he was sentenced to either jail or rehab. Elwood and Chickie go for a beer, though Elwood worries about drinking with someone fresh out of rehab.

Chickie is now living with his sister in New York and assessing his options. Elwood, on the other hand, is now the owner of a successful moving company. Elwood and Chickie reminisce about old acquaintances, although they avoid any specific mention of Nickel itself. When Chickie asks how Elwood left Nickel, Elwood is surprised. He had successfully escaped, and had hoped that the story of his escape would have become legendary to the incarcerated boys. Instead, no one remembers him, so he lies and tells

Chickie that he aged out of Nickel. When Chickie asks about Turner, Elwood changes the subject.

As they say goodbye, Chickie asks for a job. Elwood promises to consider it, but he tears up Chickie's phone number on the ride home.

Chapters 10-13 Analysis

The Nickel Boys is a bildungsroman, or coming-of-age story, that invites us to trace the evolution of Elwood through three periods of Elwood's life: his childhood and young adulthood before Nickel, his incarceration, and his life after release. The connection between younger Elwood and imprisoned Elwood is clear and linear. We can see aspects of young Elwood—deeply intelligent, brimming with idealism and the promise of social justice—in the boy who refuses to be completely beaten down by Nickel. He risks punishment to confront a bully and help a weaker student; keeps careful records about Nickel graft, hoping to expose its criminality; and has the capacity to be appalled by the stark realities Turner shows him and the simultaneous ability to declare the Christmas light display "a good job" (131).

However, the narrative features a huge break between Elwood's time in Nickel and his adulthood in New York, in both the plot (details of Elwood's escape remain sketchy) and psychology. Adult Elwood is cynical and world-weary; though he is still talented enough to have built a successful company, he recoils from the idea of helping Chickie Pete. We can't help but draw the conclusion that Nickel defeated Elwood, whose physical and psychic scars have rendered him apathetic and self-focused.

The novel allows us to draw this conclusion through its hints that victory over Earl was short-lived, since Hennepin, the man who replaced him, was much worse, and through the way Elwood eschews discussing Turner when Chickie Pete brings him up. Adult Elwood offers one image of survival: idealism turned into materialism, righteous indignation turned into prudent self-preservation. However, in retrospect, with the knowledge that adult Elwood is actually Turner, the novel appears much darker. Survivors cannot be idealists, Whitehead is saying—the promise of the young men inspired by the Civil Rights movement died in the White supremacy that resisted them. The ones left were the pragmatists who knew the system. They could engineer their own survival—maybe they could even succeed in the way that adult Elwood/Turner has—but they are not the people who could have toppled the system once and for all.

Chapter 14-Epilogue

Chapter 14 Summary

In preparation for a state inspection, the boys work to bring Nickel up to code, painting, mortaring, and cleaning. The inspection is supposed to be a surprise, but Director Hardee has access to inside information, so he can direct the boys to spend several days fixing the place up to appear as though it is up to code. Despite past allegations of abuse and several state investigations, Nickel is still in business, its reforms mostly cosmetic.

Shortly before the inspection, Elwood and Turner are charged with cleaning out the basement of Edward Childs, one of Nickel's biggest financial supporters. Childs's father had once used the basement to house Nickel boys he kept as indentured servants. While moving old junk out of the basement, Elwood confides to Turner his plan for getting rid of Nickel: give his detailed notes on Nickel's corruption to the state inspectors. Turner is furious, fearing the revelations could get them both killed; Elwood argues that simply navigating Nickel instead of rising up against it is morally wrong.

The day of the inspection, Elwood prepares to deliver his indictment to the inspection team, imagining himself a link in a chain of freedom fighters all ultimately connected to Dr. King. As the inspectors wander the grounds, Elwood tries to intercept them, but fear of undergoing another White House beating stops him. He resolves to try again, gathering courage from the promise of justice and the rule of law.

Shortly before Elwood plans to deliver his notes, Harper sends on an errand to the farm fields on the far end of campus, to tell a teacher there that the inspectors will pass by his area. By the time Elwood returns, the inspectors will be gone, but when he tries to protest to Harper, Harper coldly demands to be addressed as "Mr. Harper" and "sir."

Turner volunteers to complete the task. Given Turner's reluctance, Elwood is skeptical, but he has no choice. He hands over his records and heads to the fields. When Elwood returns, Turner tells him that he delivered the documents by placing them in a copy of the school newspaper and handing it to the inspectors. That night, Spencer and Hennepin take Elwood to the White House once again.

Chapter 15 Summary

In New York, early 2000s, Elwood has married a loving woman named Millie, who knows nothing about his experiences at Nickel. Elwood still runs Ace Moving. New York is rapidly gentrifying: Whites are moving into Harlem and appropriating Black culture and cuisine for profit. While this rankles Elwood, he appreciates the extra money they bring into the neighborhood.

While waiting for a table at a new, upscale restaurant, Elwood surveys the neighborhood, taking stock of the changes. He recognizes a building from an old moving job (removing the possessions of a deceased woman) which triggers thoughts of his own mortality. He wonders if his final memory will be of Nickel, and considers the fact that he still thinks about Nickel every single day of his life. Snapping out of this fugue, Elwood decides to buy Millie some flowers, to act the part of a more normal husband. As he is about to go get a bouquet, Millie walks up and tells him how handsome he looks.

Chapter 16 Summary

After his White House beating, Elwood is isolated in a dark cell on the third floor—one meal a day, a bucket for a toilet—another punishment that Florida has long banned but that Spencer still uses. The only reason Spencer and Hennepin didn't beat Elwood to death is that they are not sure what the results of the letter he slipped the inspectors will be. Long days there give Elwood time to consider his actions. He thinks about his hero, Dr. King, who turned his own jail time into a famous call to action, but Elwood sees only darkness. As a boy, he expected to see change soon, but it has never come. He feels his idealism slipping away.

The Florida government doesn't care about Elwood's report, which generates no follow up and thus leaves Spencer free to disappear Elwood "out back." Turner finds out about this, so he sneaks up to the third floor in the middle of the night and frees Elwood from his cell with a detailed plan for escape.

Under cover of darkness, they flee the Nickel campus and make it into town. They take bicycles from an empty house and ride toward Tallahassee. Elwood vows to bring justice down upon Spencer and the whole Nickel Academy. Riding along a main road, Turner spots a Nickel van pursuing them. They ditch the bikes, hop a fence, and run across an open pasture followed by Spencer, Hennepin, and Harper, armed with shotguns. The men fire at the fleeing boys. Hennepin misses, but Harper's shot hits Elwood, who falls into the grass. Turner escapes into nearby woods.

Epilogue Summary

In a stunning denouement, Whitehead reveals that the "Elwood" living in New York is actually Turner. After escaping, Turner took Elwood's identity—first as a way of protecting himself, and eventually as a tribute to his dead friend. Instead of a story of a daring successful escape, Turner and Elwood's flight was written up in the newspapers as a cautionary tale about dangerous fugitives.

Adult Elwood confesses the truth to Millie. He cries for hours, describing Nickel and Elwood, and showing her newspaper articles about the recent discoveries about the horrors visited on boys there. While shocked by the enormity of his lie, she understands more about his personality, his hatred of authority figures, and his dark moods. He has tried to live his life in a way that Elwood would be proud of, and Millie marvels that he has survived his past and managed to thrive. Millie also sees some aspects of her own struggles with racism as a Black woman in her husband's story, sharing her experiences being made to feel less than growing up in Virginia.

Plagued by years of guilt over giving Elwood's letter to Spencer, Turner decides to visit Nickel to confront his past and to bring some final measure of justice to his old friend. He knows that Harriet, Elwood's grandmother died a year after Elwood did; he also knows that Elwood's mother is still alive, but decides that he should be the one to give his friend a proper burial.

At the White House, a group of Nickel boys are scheduled to speak. Turner used to see these men as weak for getting together to discuss their pain; now, he realizes that his inability to ever face what happened to him is the real weakness. The novel ends with Turner looking around the hotel that used to be The Richmond Hotel—the place where Elwood kept expecting to see Black customers.

Chapter 14-Epilogue Analysis

Whitehead brings home the real tragedy of his tale with a shocking turn of events in the final chapters. All along, readers have been reading the about the horrors of Nickel with the comforting thought that at least Elwood survive— living and thriving in New York as a successful entrepreneur, he has overcome it all and succeeded against all odds. When we learn that adult Elwood is actually Turner, and that the real Elwood lies dead in a Boot Hill grave, Whitehead's narrative deception makes Elwood's fate doubly tragic. Readers have been root for this sympathetic protagonist: A smart, driven, socially engaged, unjustly convicted young man obviously does not deserve what he finds at Nickel. Finding future success seems like compensation for the injustice forced upon him, and White readers in particular may assuage their consciences with Elwood's outcome—*What he suffered is terrible, but that was then, and this is now, and society has changed enough to reward him for his pain.* Whitehead, however, does not make it that easy. There is no salvation for Elwood, no rainbow on the horizon, and the final reveal at the end of the novel hits hard. The man who deserved so much better is dead, and no amount of rationalization can erase the heartbreak.

Bringing Elwood/Turner into the present also allows Whitehead to touch upon other themes, namely gentrification. Through Turner's eyes, readers glimpse a changing New York, from 1970s decaying carcass to 2000s revitalized metropolis. Even the urban renewal angle has its dark side, however. Turner sees fellow African Americans displaced by rising property values and young Whites eager to spread their high-end urban lifestyle to cheaper areas of the city. Racism isn't a matter of isolating individual sadists like Spencer; rather, White supremacy is a system that has lived on after the legacy Jim Crow and segregation and reverberates well into the 21st century, making a mockery of America's promise of equality and freedom.

CHARACTER ANALYSIS

Elwood Curtis

Elwood is a young Black man growing up in early 1960s Florida, a segregated place where he is forever on the outside looking in. He attends a Black school (with hand-me-down textbooks from the White school), and spends his afternoons with the kitchen staff of the Whites-only hotel where his grandmother works as a maid. Elwood excels academically and believes he will see institutional change after hearing the persuasive rhetoric of Martin Luther King Jr. However, after enrolling early in a Black college through the tutelage of a politically engaged History teacher, Elwood accidentally ends up in a stolen car; his punishment is a stint at Nickel Academy, a harsh and illegally run juvenile detention center where he is tortured, abused, and otherwise traumatized.

Elwood is an optimist who is guided by a deep-seated moral code. Even during his incarceration in the senselessly violent Nickel, he tries to learn the rules so he can play by them. His commitment to fairness makes what he discovers about Nickel all the more horrifying: There are no rules; boys in Nickel are at the mercy of the sadistic savages that run the place; and there is no hope of relief since the prison fuels the local economy with graft, slave labor, and theft. It is fitting, albeit tragic, that Elwood never gives up righting wrongs. Rather than doing his best to avoid the notice of the guards, he decides to document the system around him and expose Nickel for good. His efforts fail—his report leads to his death—but there is a slight silver lining in knowing that decades later, Nickel's monstrosity will come to light.

Jack Turner

Turner, the boy whom Elwood befriends at Nickel, is a suitable foil: Unlike the idealistic and code-bound Elwood, Tuner is a true pragmatist—adaptable to the situation he finds himself and not hamstrung by ideology. Although he arguably has earned punishment in a way that Elwood really doesn't—Turner is there for throwing a brick through a car windshield—Whitehead makes Nickel such a monstrous hell that it is clear no teenage action could ever deserve such a torment. Every action has extenuating circumstances, and Turner's moment of aggression is an expression of racial sadness and shame.

In Nickel, Turner's modus operandi is to survive: He creates his own private safe space in the loft of an old warehouse, and his advice is to stay above the conflicts within Nickel to ensure personal safety. This view paints Turner as resigned to the harsh ways of the world, but also not nearly as naïve as Elwood. However, Elwood's idealism proves infectious: In the end, Turner rescues Elwood from certain death despite the threat of severe punishment and embarks on a two-person escape plan despite earlier declaring that the only real way to flee Nickel is solo.

The adult Elwood is Turner having absorbed some of Elwood's qualities, but tempering them with his own hard-earned wisdom. Turner's survival skills become entrepreneurial success, Elwood's confidence in Dr. King's vision becomes Turner's psychological stability, and, eventually, Elwood's focus on restorative justice propels Turner to return to Nickel and unburden himself of the truth of what took place there.

Harriet

Elwood's grandmother, Harriet, is a strong, but wounded, matriarch. She has seen plenty of heartbreak in her life—her father died in prison, her husband is killed in a bar fight, and her son-in-law is permanently scarred by racism. Still, when Elwood's parents abandon him for a new life on the west coast, Harriet assumes the responsibility of raising him, keeping her promising young grandson on the straight and narrow.

Harriet is wary of change, and she is skeptical of Elwood's involvement in civil rights marches. She has seen the ugly face of racism firsthand, and she deplores it, but she is also rightfully cautious about making too much noise. Elwood learns from Harriet that Black compliance in a White world is often the most prudent course of action.

Mr. Hill

Mr. Hill is Elwood's high school history teacher. Hill recognizes Elwood's potential and guides him toward self-awareness: Hill is responsible for Elwood's involvement in the Civil Rights movement and his enrollment in Melvin Griggs Technical College. Hill represents a younger generation of teachers/activists who see their job not only as passing down knowledge, but as making the next generation socially aware, a mission many colleges adhere to today.

Maynard Spencer

Spencer, the White superintendent of Nickel Academy, ostensibly is second in command to Director Hardee and the Nickel board of directors. In practice, this sadistic, racist, and vicious man runs the place entirely unchecked and unopposed. In charge of disciplining the boys, Spencer relies on immoral and illegal tactics: inducing terror, whipping boys, and killing those who still resist.

Whitehead doesn't provide a lot of psychological depth to Spencer. Instead, we see this character as a cog in the vast system that keeps places like Nickel Academy outside the reach of state law. Nickel is an enormous profit center: It earns money through the free labor of its incarcerated population, both legally, through its brickworks and printing press, and illegally, by loaning out the boys to local grandees as indentured servants, selling off state-provided supplied to local businesses, and rigging gambling on boxing matches between the boys. Spencer and his cadre of enforcers are key to making sure Nickel remains financially lucrative to the town of Eleanor—as long as the system is intact, no one will rein in his brand of monstrosity.

Harper

At first, Harper, one of the White staff members of Nickel, appears to be the foil to Spencer. Unlike Spencer's likeminded underlings Earl and Hennepin, Harper shows some measure of kindness to the boys. Having grown up at Nickel—his mother worked there—Harper feels a little kinship with the incarcerated, whom he seems to see as people. The time Turner and Elwood spend working the Community Service detail under Harper's supervision is a respite from the constant terror they experience at Nickel. The novel seems to be setting Harper up as an alternative to Spencer—a good guy who could potentially replace a bad one.

However, in one of the most stinging betrayals in a novel full of them, Harper turns out to be just as enmeshed in

Nickel's prison-industrial complex as everyone else in Eleanor. Community Service is actually the way the board of directors distribute the Nickel goods they've stolen to the town—Harper is an integral part of the system. When Elwood and Turner escape from Nickel, it is Harper who shoots and kills Elwood.

Chickie Pete

One of the most poignant foils in the novel is Chickie Pete, a Nickel boy whom the novel only introduces as an adult man. Unlike adult Elwood/Turner, Chickie Pete did not survive Nickel with his psyche intact. He struggles with alcoholism, and has not been able to hold down a job for a long time. What is most depressing for adult Elwood/Turner is that Chickie Pete has no memory of Elwood and Turner's dramatic escape from Nickel. When the men discuss their time there, we learn that adult Elwood has been buoyed by the hope that the story of their successful escape inspired hope in the other boys—in the same way that the boys were bolstered by the tale of Griff winning the boxing match against Big Chet despite being ordered to lose. Chickie Pete reveals that the escape had no such effect.

The Lingering Legacy of Slavery

The Nickel Boys chronicles the way the promise of the Civil War and the Emancipation Proclamation—the freeing of enslaved people—evolved into the racial oppression of the 1960s and beyond. The south of the 1960s, when most of the novel is set, is still the segregated south of Jim Crow laws; the system of White supremacy has found a loophole in the words of the 13th Amendment, which forbids forced labor "except as a punishment for crime." Institutions like Nickel Academy used incarceration to prop up the economic system that slavery began, extracting free labor from incarcerated boys—de facto practice of slavery but with the cover of the law. This means imprisoning as many people as possible—as Elwood's conviction shows, particularly for Black boys, even being in the vicinity of a crime is enough to guarantee being found guilty.

The system's financial disparities encourage subjugating jailed workers as much as possible—violence, abuses, and even murders of the boys are tolerated and go unpunished. Nickel Academy profits from the boys' labor as well as from administrative corruption; the punishments it inflicts are egregious and inhuman; and, while all boys are subject to abuse, the Black boys usually fare worse. Nickel's entire *modus operandi* is based on a centuries-old system that depends on a coerced, easily replaceable, and deeply unvalued workforce of disposable Black men.

The Toxicity of Lost Hope

Elwood Curtis is a canny choice for a protagonist: optimistic, smart, promising. Despite the ravages of Jim Crow, Elwood aims high. Unlike many of the other boys in his neighborhood who seem content to follow the lead of their less enterprising peers, Elwood avoids trouble, works and studies hard, and cultivates a social justice attitude. That desire for social justice remains strong despite Nickel's attempts to beat it out of him. However, as Elwood rots in solitary confinement, that hope begins to ebb, and even the inspiration of his idol, Martin Luther King Jr., is not enough to alleviate his despair. While King preaches *love thy enemy*, Elwood cannot imagine taking that leap.

The thought of forgiving and loving the men who have tortured him and robbed him of his life is impossible to contemplate. Elwood "understood neither the impulse of the proposition nor the will to execute" King's argument that Black people will win in the end by loving their oppressors (196). Had Turner never freed his friend from his dark cell on the third floor, Elwood would most likely have died within Nickel's walls, a broken man, his hope for racial equality extinguished. Even if Elwood had escaped, without his former idealism, the only thing driving him would be bitterness and anger. Although his life is cut short, he dies running toward freedom and justice and not just away from a whip. The capacity to snuff out another human being's hope is indeed one of the most toxic legacies of America's racial past.

Work as a Tool of Reform

In the United States, the idea that labor can buy freedom and the religious dogma that work signals with spiritual virtue date back centuries. These concepts united in the way early Puritans envisioned prison—as a place of redemption in which suffering might bring those incarcerated closer to God—and in the way slave owners justified slavery—as a way of elevating the inner lives of inferior peoples.

After Emancipation, prisons became institutions of forced labor under the guise of using physical hardship as religious, moral, and psychological cleansing. Under the guise of character building, Nickel boys till the fields, manufacture bricks, and run an entire printing operation, profiting Nickel's White directors while suffering deprivation, whippings, terror, and sexual abuse. There is nothing of reformative value in the boys' hard work— rather, Nickel is an institution that promotes white-collar crime, graft, and sadism.

The Power of Friendship and Racial Solidarity

Elwood, Turner, and all the Nickel boys quickly discover that one way (perhaps the only way) to survive Nickel's hellish environment is solidarity. Individually, friends not only provide necessary social contact but emotional support as well. The more experienced boys give useful advice to the "chucks" (new inmates): whom to avoid, how to earn merits, and so on. On a larger scale, solidarity is often the only unifying force among disparate personalities. The boys unite around seeing Spencer and his staff as a common enemy; and they rally around Griff as the representative of Black might, even though Griff is a merciless bully. Solidarity is protective: When Jaime poisons Earl's food, no one rats him out. They link arms, metaphorically, and present a united front until the storm passes. Without Turner, Elwood would wither away in solitary or be killed for his documenting Nickel's crimes and graft. Instead, he dies with his hope in a possible future intact—and even manages to infect his cynical friend with some measure of it. The novel ends on an act of reignited solidarity, as Turner, who has shut himself away from this kind of bonding, reconnects with other Nickel boys to speak out about what they underwent.

SYMBOLS AND MOTIFS

Martin Luther King at Zion Hill

Elwood's record album of King's stirring oratory is indispensable to his emotional growth. It fills him with idealism when he is surrounded by injustice, and it lays the groundwork for his participation in a Civil Rights march. King's words represent a vision of racial equity, an ideal that serves as a life preserver for Elwood in Nickel's flagrant racism.

While King's (and Elwood's) optimism appear quaint and naïve to Turner, he is ultimately swayed enough to risk his life for the *possibility* of justice. Even after Elwood dies and Turner assumes his identity, he, Turner, tries to atone for his betrayal of Elwood by living the life he feels Elwood deserves, a life that honors King's powerful message of love and transcendence.

Christmas Lights

Nickel's Christmas display is renowned statewide. People come from all over Florida and neighboring states to view the spectacle. Although the boys do all the work of hanging lights and assembling displays, they receive little credit. Yet, despite this, the boys take pride in their work. They see hope for something better in the flashing lights. As Turner and Elwood sit on a hill and observe the pageantry, Elwood comments, "We did good" (131).

The thousands of twinkling lights are beacons of hope for all of the Nickel boys. The image of light eradicating darkness is a potent one, and Elwood sees in the spectacle the hope that one day the darkness of racism will retreat before the light of tolerance.

Elwood's Journal

When Elwood is assigned to Community Service detail—a cover for delivering stolen goods all over the town of Eleanor—the first thing Turner tells him is to keep him mouth shut. Shocked by the flagrant illegality he witnesses, Elwood keeps detailed records in a journal on every delivery he and Turner make. Spurred by his earlier success in getting a letter published in an activist newspaper, Elwood believes this journal will expose wrongdoing at Nickel and free him and the other boys.

The journal represents Elwood's trust in a fair and just world, the kind Martin Luther King Jr. described: "The moral arc of the universe is long, but it bends toward justice." In such a world, Elwood could take down the entire Nickel apparatus if only good White people know the truth. Of course, what Elwood doesn't realize is just how deeply Nickel is embedded in a self-perpetuating, White supremacist, financially lucrative system. The reckoning that comes is lackluster at best—decades too late, too meager to punish anyone involved, and with little recompense for victims besides a small measure of healing.

The Iron Rings

Beyond Nickel's laundry and the horse stables sit two large oak trees with an iron ring pounded into each one. Rings like these are a staple of concentration camps as well as southern plantations. At Nickel, they are called "out back," and are where Spencer takes boys for the most severe punishment—a horsewhipping that usually lands the boy in an unmarked grave. The idea that Spencer can disappear boys who go against him or defy White authority with no repercussions and with complete impunity is the logical, monstrously horrific, endpoint of the system Nickel has created. They represent the brutal punishments meted out to anyone who would.

Fun Town

In his Zion Hill speech, Martin Luther King, Jr. describes Fun Town, the segregated amusement park his daughter Yolanda is barred from, in one kinetic image. Its flashing lights, speeding roller coasters, wide-eyed excitement highlight the unnecessary unfairness of segregation. How does one explain injustice to a Black child who wants to ride a roller coaster without tarnishing that child's innocence and hope? Hearing Dr. King tell Yolanda, "you are as good as anybody that goes into Fun Town" (12) gives Elwood hope that one day, he will experience the same thrills the White children do. Whitehead returns to this image throughout the novel. For example, the Christmas lights display at Nickel reminds Elwood of Fun Town commercials of the rocket ship ride, and he imagines strapping himself into such a ship and flying off to the stars, to a world he can't see yet but one he hopes to one day.

IMPORTANT QUOTES

1. "Even in death the boys were trouble." (Prologue, Page 3)

   Whitehead's opening sentence signals something ominous, but also strangely hopeful. The "boys" are, in death, stirring up bad forgotten memories. This trouble, however, is righteous trouble, the kind of trouble former U.S. Representative John Lewis would label "good" and "necessary," for it is only through the trouble of waking long dead ghosts that Nickel's past sins are brought to light.

2. "Explain the misguided thinking of some whites—not all whites, but enough whites—that gave it force and meaning." (Chapter 1, Page 12)

   Elwood imagines a conversation between Dr. King and his young daughter, Yolanda, in which he must explain to her why she can't enter Fun Town, a local amusement park. Careful not to condemn all White people, King must nevertheless concede that those who don't agree with—but don't take an active stand against—institutions like segregation are giving tacit support by refusing to raise their voices in protest.

3. "To see him from across the street—the serious young lad heaving his freight of the world's knowledge—was to witness a scene that might have been illustrated by Norman Rockwell, if Elwood had had white skin." (Chapter 1, Page 16)

   For Elwood, knowledge is a beacon of hope, a passport to the world beyond Tallahassee, so when he finds a set of encyclopedias at the hotel where Harriet works, he can't wait to dive into their pages. It is an adorable image—a young boy, lugging a set of books, eager for knowledge—but as Whitehead points out, the Norman Rockwell painting that would capture this image would necessarily portray the boy as White. To challenge that assumption is to acknowledge every preconceived notion about race and learning and aspiration.

4. "Elwood asked his grandmother when Negroes were going to start staying at the Richmond and she said it's one thing to tell someone to do what's right and another thing for them to do it." (Chapter 2, Page 18)

Herein lies the fundamental problem. More than a century after The Emancipation Proclamation, decades after the end of Jim Crow, why does racial injustice persist? Changing the law is one thing, a necessary first step, but changing attitudes is something else entirely.

5. "Young knights taking the fight to dragons." (Chapter 2, Page 22)

As Elwood sees news footage of protests and sit-ins and looks for his own place in the Civil Rights Movement, he is afraid. To watch young people marching for their rights and getting beaten and bloodied in the process is frightening; he assuages his fear by romanticizing the marchers, imagining them as mythic figures caught up in a more traditional kind of epic struggle. Visualizing the struggle in this way gives Elwood the fortitude to don his own armor, pick up his own broadsword, and join the fight.

6. "Letting the kids steal was almost an investment, the way he looked at it." (Chapter 2, Page 25)

Elwood's boss, Mr. Marconi, has a curiously laid-back attitude about shoplifting from his store. He looks the other way, figuring that if he calls out every kid who steals a candy bar, he'll be seen as an authoritative White man, and he'll lose business in the mostly Black neighborhood. Elwood, called to a code of honor by the inspiring speeches of Martin Luther King, takes great offense at the shoplifting. For Marconi, "letting the kids steal" is an economic investment in the future; for Elwood, it's accepting lowered expectations and undignified stereotype. This ideological conflict foreshadows Elwood's experiences at Nickel.

7. "They beat him up and tore his clothes and didn't understand why wanted to protect a white man." (Chapter 2, Page 27)

   Is Marconi a kindly, tolerant man, or is part of the White supremacist system, needing to be prodded to stock Black media that will appeal to his customers? Is he both? Elwood struggles with the concept that even White people who are individually benign, or even positive, cannot help perpetuating the racist system they are embedded in. As a child, Elwood cannot see the larger system at work; instead, he defends the tobacco shop because not doing so was to undermine his own dignity" (27). Only at Nickel will he realize the larger forces at play.

8. "They'd set off down one road at the beginning of class and it always led back to their doorsteps." (Chapter 3, Page 30)

   Elwood's History teacher, Mr. Hill, has a gift for making history relevant. Although the class focuses on American History since the Civil War, Hill always illustrates the ways in which the past has led to the present, how the deeds of their forebears inform their current reality. Further, he has the real-world experience that lends credibility to his lessons: scars and tales from his own participation in the Civil Rights Movement.

9. "Act above your station, and you will pay." (Chapter 3, Page 33)

   Harriet's take-away from her brief, reluctant participation in the Civil Rights Movement—a bus boycott—is that Black people must learn their place. Wresting power away from those who hold it never ends well.

10. "At the demonstrations he had felt somehow *closer* to himself." (Chapter 3, Page 37)

    After Elwood attends his first protest march, he finds camaraderie with other kindred spirits—adults and older students who all share the same vision of equality. This closeness resonates deeply; it gives him a mission and an ethos that helps him through the worst of Nickel's abuses and pushes him to try to expose and dismantle the Academy.

11. "The officer told the white boys that they were sitting with a car thief and Bill laughed. 'Oh, I used to go joy-riding all the time,' he said." (Chapter 4, Page 47)

    Elwood is transported to Nickel with two White offenders who exemplify a hard lesson in the unequal application of the law. He was convicted for simply being in the proximity of a crime, while the White boy boasts about getting away with the same infraction multiple times.

12. "He'd learn that most of the kids had been sent here for much lesser—and nebulous and inexplicable—offenses." (Chapter 4, Page 53)

    Kids are sent to a place like Nickel ostensibly for character and attitude correction: Elwood is told that he is lucky to be sent to a reform school rather than prison for such a major crime as car theft. However, Nickel is an early example of the prison-industrial complex: an institution with a financial stake in getting and keeping as many kids prisoner as possible.

13. "Everybody back home knew him as even, dependable—Nickel would soon understand that about him, too." (Chapter 5, Page 64)

    Elwood resolves to survive Nickel the only way he knows how: to let his character speak for itself. His diligence and work ethic have always won him favor in school and at work, so he sees no reason it won't work here. Elwood, however, soon discovers that Nickel follows no logic. Despite his best efforts to stay out of trouble, he learns that at Nickel, trouble has a way of seeking Black boys out.

14. "'Wow, they got you good,' Dr. Cooke said whenever he changed Elwood's dressings." (Chapter 7, Page 74)

    After Elwood's beating, he is sent to the infirmary to recover. In a heartless display of bedside manner, Nickel's resident physician makes light of Elwood's injuries. Perhaps Cooke has seen too many of these injuries to be sympathetic anymore; or perhaps he believes that beatings build character. However, the care which Cooke and his nurse lavish upon an unseen White patient suggests that, deep down, the doctor believes that, as a Black boy, Elwood deserves it.

15. "More than once Elwood caught himself swinging the scythe with too much violence, like he was attacking the grass with a leather strap." (Chapter 8, Page 84)

    Elwood, by any measure a gentle boy, finds his actions propelled by anger. Powerless in the face of horrific abuse, he vents his frustration on the landscape. Abuse rarely corrects behavior; it merely perpetuates abuse; and the image of Elwood swinging a scythe is portentous—a haunting image of Death itself.

16. "Some names took a while to fill in, but Elwood had always been the patient type, and thorough." (Chapter 8, Page 96)

    As Elwood works with Turner in the Community Service detail, he finally finds a use for his talents. Keeping meticulous records of all Community Service deliveries, Elwood gathers evidence of institutional corruption that he hopes will topple Spencer and his administration and provide justice for all those who have suffered under its yoke. The plan gives him a purpose, a battle to wage in place of a protest march.

17. "Any time a white man asked you about yourself, they were about to fuck you over." (Chapter 9, Page 102)

    Overhearing Spencer order Griff to throw the fight with Big Chet in the third round, Turner understands from the beginning that Spencer has something devious in mind. Spencer's friendliness could never be anything but a pretense. Despite Griff's attempt to comply, he misunderstands the instructions and pays with his life.

18. "Like justice, it existed in theory." (Chapter 10, Page 118)

    Jaime, the Latino boy who shuttles back and forth between the White and Black campuses, avoids trouble by playing by the rules Elwood can't quite grasp. For many of the Nickel boys, justice is a grand concept from soaring rhetoric that rhetoric doesn't exist in practice.

19. "But there it was before him, pointed at the stars, decked in a hundred flickering lights, waiting for takeoff: a rocket. Launched in darkness toward another dark planet they couldn't see." (Chapter 10, Page 131)

    Gazing out at the Christmas decorations, Elwood has a vision of the rocket as both amusement park ride and time machine. He remembers the rides at Fun Town, the Whites-only amusement park, wondering if the day will ever come when he can enjoy the park—a child's benchmark of racial equity. He also sees the rocket pointing to a better future for all Black people, covering not distance, but time, the only thing that can ultimately undo centuries of oppression.

20. "It was terrible out there. But it was good for the rest of the city to see what kind of place they were really living in." (Chapter 11, Page 141)

    Living in New York City during a summer garbage strike equalizes the experience for all New Yorkers, both Black and White. Everyone walks the same streets, smells the same rotting garbage, dodges the same hungry rats. This gives Elwood (Turner) some measure of hope that those in power will correct the systemic problems affecting New York's poorest, mostly Black and Latino, residents. Cities, however, like institutions, grind on relentlessly, apathetic to the needs of their citizens.

21. "It was crazy to run and crazy not to run." (Chapter 12, Page 146)

    Nickel boys are faced with an impossible dilemma. Their prison relies on fear of reprisal and helplessness —there are no walls or bars around the campus, but where would an escaping boy go? To gaze out at the free world is almost too enticing, and more than one boy has formulated a foolproof escape plan, only to be caught, punished, and laid to rest in an unmarked grave.

22. "He was like one of those Negroes Dr. King spoke of in his letter from jail, so complacent and sleepy after years of oppression that they had adjusted to it and learned to sleep in it as their only bed." (Chapter 12, Page 156)

    Still haunted by his beating, Elwood plays by the rules and avoids trouble; but his compliance takes its toll: He forfeits his dignity by "stopping fighting." When Elwood awakens from his emotional slumber, he begins to formulate his plan for justice and escape.

23. "All those lost geniuses—sure not all of them were geniuses, Chickie Pete for example was not solving special relativity—but they had been denied even the simple pleasure of being ordinary." (Chapter 13, Page 166)

Turner, now living in New York as Elwood, reflects on a fellow Nickel boy Chickie Pete's lost musical talent. He might have played professionally, but Nickel has slammed that window of opportunity shut. How many other boys, he wonders, might have had bright futures had they not spent time in Nickel? Even those boys who had no special talent were robbed of the simple joys of life.

24. "The capacity to suffer. Elwood—al the Nickel boys—existed in that capacity." (Chapter 14, Page 172)

    Elwood, locked in solitary confinement, reflects on the words of Dr. King: "[W]e will wear you down by our capacity to suffer" (172). for the first time in his life, Elwood questions King's demand that his people suffer the insufferable. Surviving Nickel is a marathon endurance contest; and while Dr. King might exhort his followers to persevere in spite of the pain, Elwood feels himself filling up with only despair. The capacity to suffer is "an impossible thing" (173) to ask.

25. "The lie was big but she understood it, given how the world had crumpled him up, the more she took in his story." (Epilogue, Page 206)

    When Turner confesses his true identity to his wife, Millie, after years of marriage, she is shocked at first; but as he tells her about his experience in Nickel, she understands and forgives. She recognizes how much his childhood has squashed the psyche of her husband, a man who, despite the odds against him, has persevered and succeeded. Turner's honesty and resilience transcend his lies.

ESSAY TOPICS

1. Racism is often subtle and insidious. What are some of the less obvious ways racism affects Elwood, Turner, and Harriet?

2. Initially, Elwood wants to follow the rules and get out of Nickel unscathed, but finds it impossible. Is he right that there is no logic to how Nickel works, or does he miss cues about how to avoid trouble? Why or why not?

3. How do Nickel's racist practices perpetuate terror in the boys?

4. Elwood is industrious, smart, and hardworking. How would the novel be different if Whitehead's protagonist had been one of the tobacco shop thieves? What about Griff or Corey? Does it matter that Elwood is innocent and admirable? Why or why not?

5. Research modern reform schools and compare current practices to Nickel. What has changed? What remains the same?

6. Why does Whitehead toggle back and forth between past and present in Part 3 of the novel?

7. Harriet believes that Black people who strive for equality will be met with harsh opposition from the White establishment for daring to "act above your station" (33). Does the novel agree? Why or why not?

8. Why does Whitehead include descriptions of Nickel's financial ties to the town of Eleanor?

9. Spencer is an obviously evil figure. However, Nickel Academy operates for decades despite state inspections. Who is ultimately to blame for Nickel's continuing abuses? Why?

10. Turner appropriates Elwood's identity to give his friend the life he could never have. Is it enough? Does Turner's final trip to Tallahassee provide adequate closure?

Made in the USA
Columbia, SC
17 August 2023

21761530R00030